Art & Science Collaborations:

Communicating Climate Change

Eilidh Guthrie

An imprint of Boom Publications Ltd

272 Bath Street
Glasgow SCOTLAND
G2 4JR

Boom Graduates and the logo are trademarks of Boom Publications Ltd.

Boom Publications Ltd is a more-than-profit company, dedicating over half our profits to university scholarships for underprivileged students worldwide. In order to offset our carbon footprint, we also pledge to plant a tree for each graduation book commissioned.

Art & Science Collaborations: Communicating Climate Change
was first published in Great Britain in 2022.

Copyright © Eilidh Guthrie. Eilidh Guthrie has asserted her right under the
Copyright, Designs and Patents Act, 1988,
to be identified as Author of this work.
For legal purposes any Acknowledgements constitute
an extension of this copyright page.
Cover design by Boom Graduates Ltd and the Book Cover Zone USA.

All rights are reserved. No part of this publication may be reproduced or transmitted in any form or by any means, electronic or mechanical, including photocopying, recording, or any information storage or retrieval system, without prior permission in writing from the publishers.

Boom Publications Ltd do not have any control over, or responsibility for any third-party websites referred to or in this book. All internet addresses given in this book were correct at the time of going to press. The author and publisher regret any inconvenience if addresses have changed or sites have ceased to exist, but can accept no responsibility for any such changes.

Typeset by Helen at Boom Graduates.
Printed and bound in the UK.

To find out more about our authors and books visit www.boomgraduates.com
and sign up for our newsletters.

Art & Science Collaborations

We plant a tree for every
Boom Graduate book commissioned, and
thereafter plant a tree for every 10 books sold.

THG
(more : trees)

MEMBER

Watch our forest grow at
https://moretrees.eco/forest/BoomPublicationsLtd/

Eilidh Guthrie

Art & Science Collaborations

Art & Science Collaborations:

Communicating Climate Change

Eilidh Guthrie

Contents

Author biography..9
Abstract..11
Introduction..13
Science and Society..15
Boundary Objects 23
Adaptation Projects..41
Conclusion..59
References...63
Artist's images 71
Acknowledgements 91
BOOM! 93
A note about Boom Graduates...95
Notes 99

Eilidh Guthrie

Author biography

Eilidh Guthrie is a fine art graduate from DJCAD whose art practice draws inspiration from our natural world. She is passionate about how art can visualise scientific data in a more experiential and interesting way, especially in reference to climate change.

Eilidh Guthrie

Abstract

In this book in the context of climate change, I examine the interaction between science and society, including scepticism and biased assimilation. I look at how art and science collaborate and how information is transferred between the two discourses. I look at how adaption efforts using art and science might either reinforce or lessen the psychological obstacles we confront when thinking about climate change. My methodology consists of primary research resources including statistical data about society's connection with climate science and the artwork case studies which I use for discussion. I also look for secondary sources, such as scholarly literature on the issue of artworks with a climate change theme, such as books or internet articles. I discovered that there is a communication gap between science and society as a result of the public's lack of scientific understanding and biased assimilation. During my exploration, I come across the theory of 'boundary objects' between artists and scientists during collaborations that include syntactic, semantic and pragmatic boundary objects. These collaborations can explore multiple scenarios of a post-climate change world including individual survival methods or community based hypothesises. Concluding this paper, I argue that art and science collaborations about climate change should portray positive, wellbeing focused futures - these will be the most engaging to the public and will break down the psychological barriers including 'distance' and 'doom'.

Introduction

Living in the Anthropocene, the news continuously broadcasts climate change statistics and graphs, information that may be difficult to understand unless you are a scientist, and data which can also strengthen the psychological barriers we face when thinking about global warming. To help bridge the communication gap between science and society, we can experience art and science collaborations. Throughout this book, I explore boundary objects that occur during these said collaborations and how each of them is a varied relationship of knowledge between the two discourses. I examine the theory of risk perception and availability, heuristic as they can be, applied to climate change artworks. They can tell us how the knowledge presented can be accepted or rejected, depending on each individual's beliefs.

Firstly, I analyse the relationship between society and science referring to scepticism and biased assimilation in the context of climate change. Following this, I discuss several case studies of art and science collaborations and what type of boundary objects they are. Lastly, I review art and science collaborations that propose adaption to climate change. Depending on how these futures are visualised results in varied engagement by the public.

Science and Society

Art has faced humanity's most demanding situations including war, inequality, and ailment, creating spaces for aching, asking questions, conforming and solutions. We are currently enduring an Anthropocene extinction and global warming is humankind's greatest threat. Statistics from the UK's 2020 carbon emissions show we are halfway to reaching net-zero, however, this was due to nationwide lockdowns, and it is likely to begin to rise again in 2022 (Carbon Brief, 2021). While there is increasing awareness about climate change as it starts to become a reality (increasing natural disasters, rising sea levels broadcast in the news), there is still a barrier between scientists and non-scientists. In a study by the Public Attitudes to Science in 2019, 49% of the participants felt that scientists put too little effort into informing the public, and 38% saw scientists as being poor communicators (Department for Business, Energy, and

Industrial Strategy, 2019). This distance in communication between scientists and society requires another medium to bridge the gap and transfer important knowledge to non-scientists. This medium can be any artistic practice, including sculpture, installation, film, and sound work.

When exploring the relationship between science and society we can look at the deficit model. The information deficit hypothesis (also known as the scientific literacy/knowledge deficit model) blames public scepticism or hostility toward science and technology on a lack of understanding caused by a lack of information in studies of public comprehension of science (Pouliot and Godbout, 2014, p. 833). David Dickson, a scientific journalist argues that social scientists created the term in the 1980s, although the original definition was "not to describe a mode of scientific communication" which is how the term has been known in recent times (Dickson, 2005). Dickson states that a belief of the IDM (information deficit model) is that to reduce public scepticism, better information must be provided. Education can be a major factor towards this deficit, with degree-educated individuals (42% compared to just 1% without a degree) among the demographic categories with the greatest proportions with strong scientific understanding (Department for Business, Energy, and Industrial Strategy, 2019). When looking at the public's perception of climate change, we might consider biased assimilation. When new data is perceived in such a manner that it is assimilated into prior preconceptions and expectations, this is known as biased assimilation. Introduced by scientists at Stanford University, they described the public analysing evidence in a biased manner as *'they are apt to accept "confirming" evidence at face value while subjecting "disconfirming" evidence to critical evaluation, and, as a result, draw undue support for their initial positions from mixed or random findings'* (Lord et al, 1979, p. 2099). This prejudice is not always intentional, and individuals tend to question the motivations of those who do not agree with them, making it tough to overcome. If an individual has strong feelings about global warming, they are more inclined to accept or reject evidence that confirms or contradicts their preexisting ideas. The School of Psychology at the University of Cardiff conducted an experimental study to measure the participant's scepticism regarding global warming before and after reading two media articles that made contrasting statements regarding climate change's reality and severity (designed to give rise to uncertainty). The findings show that people with competing views on climate change process new, contradictory information regarding climate change in a biased manner. When participants were divided into two groups ('sceptical' and 'non-sceptical'), they rated two editorials positing conflicting views concerning climate change differently. Participants appeared to rate the editorials' persuasiveness and reliability based on their prior attitudes: those with more previous scepticism about global warming rated the sceptical paper as more convincing and credible than the pro-climate crisis article (and vice versa for those with less scepticism) (Corner, et al, 2012, p 476) This factor can be considered when investigating art and science collaborations. While artworks about climate may aid an individual's opinion about the seriousness of the climate crisis, the artworks may also support the scepticism of another who doubts that global warming is a consequential threat to human existence. Per Espen Stoknes, a philosopher, and Green Party member, calls the psychological barriers that we face on the topic of climate change the *'five D's'* (Stoknes, 2015, p. 82), which are *'Distance // Doom // Dissonance // Denial // iDentity'*. These are the five defence barriers that block climate messages and these elements may seem impenetrable when seen as a whole. They are connected, yet they are still separate. Our identity affects our thinking about climate change as we encounter opposition to proposals for identity transformation, and we experience denial, so we do not feel criticised for our lifestyle choices. Dissonance is a barrier as we still have harmful lifestyles when we know they badly affect our planet. We undergo a doom barrier because we would rather not think about a frightening, apocalyptic future. Lastly, we have a 'distance' barrier that blocks engagement with climate change; we cannot see global warming as it is distanced far away. This distance can mean climate change is located where we cannot see it, for example, glacier ice caps melting, most of us do not experience these effects. This distance can also be related to time – the worst impacts of climate change is not in an individual's lifetime. Stoknes tells us to see the *'five D's'* as concentric rings around the citadel of the individual, with distance serving as the first barrier of protection and identification serving as the ultimate, deepest level of defence (Stoknes, 2015, p. 83). Identity, which is linked to biased assimilation, is the most interior psychological obstacle. Stoknes then goes on to remark that in its fight against climate science, the anti-climate movement has succeeded in breaking down each of these hurdles (Stoknes, 2015, p.84). However, climate communicators, for example, have unintentionally triggered them by communicating climate data via abstract graphics and lengthy paragraphs, failing to link dangers to action possibilities, dependence on poor communication, and unneeded polarisation promoting ego and risk perception. The *'five D's* is an important concept to consider when communicating climate change as it tells us why the public wishes to shut down conversations about climate change. It also tells us that to reach the deepest defence (identity), we must first break down the barrier of 'distance 'and 'doom', and art and science collaborations can help break these defences. Depending on how global warming is communicated can dictate how the individual receives the information. Using art as a tool can transfer the data to the public in an accessible fashion, dismantling phycological barriers. Artworks with environmental themes can make climate change appear less distant and they can suggest adaptation to climate change and hope, therefore tackling two psychological barriers.

Eilidh Guthrie

Boundary Objects

When researching art-science partnerships, it is important to consider that art-science crossovers are portrayed as an endeavour to bring two separate cultures together. This may be traced to C.P. Snow's lecture, 'Two Cultures', presented in 1959. In his lecture, C.P. Snow (1959, p. 4) stated that the sciences and humanities had become dangerously divided, with one speciality having little comprehension of the other. While this talk was intended to demonstrate that science and technology studies were superior to the arts, his fundamental framing of the arts-science divide became the argument for which he is most remembered and quoted within the arts-science discourse. This lecture was characterised as *'an earnest plea for intercommunication across the high table, as between exponents of the scientific and humanistic disciplines'* (Levin, 1965, p. 2) by Harry Levin, an American literary critic. By working across the arts and sciences, this polemic was discussed and accepted as a viable place for creative endeavours - we may discover new views, new areas for creativity, and perhaps even new disciplinary fusion. Sixty years on from C.P. Snow's lecture, there is no longer a scientist versus humanist argument, the two are no longer seen as incompatible. Within this context, artists can collaborate with scientists, to produce experiential and informative works that can educate and inspire the public about climate change. Art and science are different social worlds, but collaboration between these two disciplines can produce '*boundary objects*' (Star and Griesemer, 1989, p. 392) that enable the transference of knowledge between each subject. The concept of a boundary object is a highly valuable theoretical tool that many fields have embraced such as computer science and information science. Looking at complicated circumstances through the perspective of boundary objects might help us see how diverse individuals can work together on a project while having distinct and frequently competing interests. Star and Griesemer discuss that scientific activity is heterogeneous and, to be effective, it needs collaboration among many actors (Star and Griesemer, 1989, p. 392). The form of boundary objects was described as:

> *Objects which are both plastic enough to adapt to local needs and the constraints of the several parties employing them, yet robust enough to maintain a common identity across sites'*

(Star and Griesemer, 1989, p. 393)

Boundary items such as specimens, field notes, and standardised forms, were mentioned in the context of the Museum of Vertebrate Zoology in Star and Griesemer's article (Star and Griesemer, 1989, p. 406). Other examples of boundary objects can be geographical maps, museums, diagrams and of course, artworks. Science studies the natural world via controlled experimentation, categorisation, and analysis, while art is interested in examining the human existence through analogy, metaphor, critique, and judgement (Cross, 1982, p. 222). Art emphasises subjectivity, imagination, and originality whereas science stresses objectivity, reason, and neutrality. Collaborations between art and science can generate visuals and objects that represent complex scientific information while also making it accessible to a broad audience. Boundary objects can be used to help scientists experience different ways of communicating climate change to the public. Professor of learning and teaching Chantal Pouliot, and scientist Julie Godbout state that:

> *Articles in scientific journals mostly aim at informing other scientists; and scientific conferences and symposia are attended only by scientists and scientific editors. We therefore think that the most effective way to help scientists think outside the box is to introduce a curricular component that presents the alternative models and engages the budding researchers in learning and debating the subject.*
>
> (Pouliot and Godbout, 2014, p. 835)

Recognising the general public's reluctance to engage with scientific texts that Pouliot and Godbout highlight, they introduce the concept of NEUVis as another form of communication. The term NEUVis: Non-Expert User Visualisation, is used to describe the visual depiction of scientific data for a general audience (Gough, et al., 2014, p. 335). These NEUVis are created by indirect or direct partnerships in which scientific information is passed from a domain specialist, such as a climatologist, to a non-expert user, public, or instructor to a student cohort (Gough, et al, 2016, p. 19). They are one-off visualisations for the public who does not have specialist expertise in the subject from which the data was derived. Returning to the topic of boundary objects, two can be addressed in the context of creating resiliency to climate change via creative NEUVis. The conversation between three social groups, scientists, artists, and the public, spans two borders. For the construction of visualisation, the first boundary object is between scientists and creative practitioners. This must be worked out so that the artist can accurately convey the results of scientific study in a manner that allows the audience to interact with the facts on several levels. The audience is on one side of the second boundary object, while the creative practitioner and scientist are on the other. In this approach, the work itself functions as a translator on the scientist's behalf. Paul Carlile discusses two sorts of boundary objects before introducing a third. They are referred to as *'syntactic', 'semantic'* and *'pragmatic'*. *Syntactic* (Carlile, 2002, p. 443) border objects are knowledge archives that give access to the information without requiring direct cooperation; the artist employs this approach to get scientific material without requiring direct collaboration, sometimes resulting in an indirect collaboration. The s*emantic* (Carlile, 2002, p. 444) barrier draws attention to the disparities and helps collaborators to comprehend the other group's source of information. Lastly, there is the *pragmatic* approach, which.

> *Highlights the importance of understanding the consequences that exist between things that are different and dependent on each other.*
>
> (Carlile, 2002, p. 445)

More than merely realising that there is a difference separating them, the pragmatic approach promotes the understanding of each group's knowledge. Throughout this book, I will be referencing artworks within the context of climate change and will discuss which type of boundary object was used. Each kind of boundary object facilitates communication differently between the two discourses and this then represents knowledge and make the knowledge more learnable. In turn, to resolve a boundary between art and science, the knowledge is transformed and opens space for innovation. Star and Greisemer (1986, p. 393) suggest that boundary objects can be abstract or concrete, they are tangible for each collaboration. These definitions can inform us of how that knowledge was transferred and transformed during a partnership between art and science and highlights how the function of the artwork dictates which type of boundary object is best suited.

When discussing art and science collaborations, the artist led organisation Cape Farewell must be honourably mentioned. Cape Farewell serves as a catalyst, facilitating collaboration between artists, scientists, and communities. The initiatives emphasise humanity's harmful influence on the environment and urge people to act toward a sustainable cultural transformation by making art based on scientific reality. David Buckland, the founder of Cape Farewell, describes this method of communication as *'perhaps cultural approaches can succeed where the hard facts of science have failed'* (Buckland, 2012, p. 137). Supported by Cape Farewell, the *Pollution Pods* (Pinsky, 2017) was created as part of Climart, an interdisciplinary and worldwide research project that united environmental psychologists, natural scientists, and artists to look at how environmental art may be used to raise concerns about climate change. The artwork comprises of a frame constructed of salvaged Norwegian wood on the outside. A PVC bio - based plastic membrane is suspended from this. Within the Pods, pollution is carefully replicated in a variety of different ways, using humidifiers, haze producers, smell diffusers, fans, and an ozone machine, heaters and air conditioners control the temperature and humidity. This artwork compares five distinct worldwide habitats where the quality of air, ozone, nitrogen dioxide, carbon monoxide and sulphur dioxide levels of five cities are replicated using a series of climatically regulated pods. Audiences are taken through the incredible haze and pollution of London, New Delhi, Beijing, and Sao Paolo, starting with the extremely pristine air of Tautra in Norway.

One of the collaborators of this project, artist Michael Pinsky described the work:

> *The experience of walking through the pollution pods demonstrates that these worlds are interconnected and interdependent. Our need for ever cheaper goods is reflected in the ill-health of many people in world and in the ill-health of our planet as a whole. In this installation we can feel, taste and smell the environments that are the norm for a huge swathe of the world's population.*

Perhaps the visceral memory of these toxic places will make us think again before we buy something else we don't really need.

(Pinsky, 2017)

This installation highlights the unquenchable thirst of capitalist consomption as the source of pollution. People in China and India are harmed by airborne poisons manufactured by factories completing orders from the West, while we in the developed countries live in an atmosphere with comparatively pure air. The production of this work facilitated a *semantic* boundary object, where both collaborators understand the knowledge source of the other group, for example: before deciding to design the PPs, the team reviewed the gap between the public and climate change, and whether it was reasonable to change the display, focusing on past research on climate change and air pollution communication (Pinsky, 2017). The visitors would not be able to smell the global warming gases, that gases that has been the major focus of climate scientists and policymakers, it was ruled irrational to add gases that contribute to the greenhouse effect to the pods (i.e., carbon dioxide and methane). By using unharmful gases that you can smell and taste, the experience of the installation was more powerful. The creators of this installation hope that the public encounter with this work will encourage them to think about how they contribute to capitalism and how their individual choices can add to greenhouse gas emissions. (Pinksy and Sommer, 2020, p.95).

Using art as a tool to communicate climate change issues is a unique way to register both modes of thinking: cognitive engagement and emotional engagement. According to social scientist Robert Zajonc's psychological theories of risk perception, emotions *'often arise prior to cognition and play a crucial role in subsequent rational thought'* (Zajonc, 1980, cited in Leiserowitz, 2006, p. 47). Awareness is influenced by two simultaneous and interacting forms of information processing: an analytic, rational, cognitive system and an experiential, emotionally motivated system (Epstein, 1994, p. 714). Changes in behaviour would not occur without both styles of thinking, according to findings from social psychology-based climate communication research. (Lorenzoni et al., 2007, p. 446). For example, within the UK, there is a high level of public awareness about climate change and there is government funded campaigning about carbon emissions (analytic information), but there is still not a lot of behavioural change relating to low-carbon practices. It can be suggested that these campaigns fail because they disregard emotional engagement, and for some people climate change appears too distant to them, distance being one of the psychological barriers that individuals experience when faced with climate knowledge (Spence et al, 2012, p. 958). Psychological distance has four dimensions – geographical, temporal, distance between the social target and the individual, and scepticism (Liberman and Trope, 2008, p. 2). Climate change appears distant on all these factors (Milfont, 2010, pp. 12 13) thus it is important for other modes of communication to break this barrier for climate change to be engaging to the public. As Art engages the experiential system, art is comprehensive, emotive, and intuitive, encoding reality in tangible pictures, metaphors, and stories. Art can trigger emotions in the viewer, as lecturer of philosophy Nicholas J Bullot tells us that *'to act as artistic and political catalysts of environmental change, artists can contribute to (i) the public's epistemic and emotional sensitivity to environmental issues and (ii) the publics cooperative action on and reflective thinking about the environment'* (Bullot, 2014, p. 512). Professor of psychology, Seymour Epstein states that *'experientially derived knowledge is often more compelling and more likely to influence behaviour than is abstract knowledge'* (Epstein, 1994, p. 711) thus it can be suggested that experiencing an artwork about climate change can motivate behavioural changes more than viewing scientific data.

Art and science partnerships can focus on any element of climate change such as rising sea levels, pollution, habitat loss, climate racism, and mass extinction. It can especially be effective to exhibit changes in our environment from global warming that we cannot see, such as coral bleaching. *Reefs on the Edge* (de Bérigny, 2011) is a creative interactive exhibit that raises awareness of the impact of climate change on marine habitats. Media artist and researcher Caitilin de Bérigny created the artwork in partnership with Dr Erica Woolsey, a marine biologist who examined the long-term impact of rising sea temperatures on coral embryo. It was created using scientific data, underwater photos, video footage, and audio taken at the Great Barrier Reef's One Tree Island Reef. Other collaborators study the Master of Interaction Design and Electronic Arts, including artists Phillip Gough and Adityo Pratomo, who created and developed an interactive display that depicted scientific findings; Ge Wu who was responsible for editing the multi-channel video installation. Using sounds recorded in a natural reef environment, Michael Bates edited these recordings to create the soundscape for the installation (de Bérigny et al., 2011, p. 454).

This installation depicts hypothetical outcomes for coral reefs, urging people to learn more about climate change's consequences. The year of 2020 was described as *'one of the worst coral bleaching years in history'* (Goreau, et al., 2021, p. 1140) due to the rising temperatures of the air and sea, and the ocean becoming more acidic. The study for this artwork looked at the survival of juvenile coral on the Great Barrier Reef, and it concluded that rising sea temperature would impede coral development and put reef ecosystems at risk. (Woolsey, 2012, p. 4). The artist went on two field excursions with the scientists to acquire underwater video and pictures for the artwork as part of this partnership. (Gough et al, 2016, p. 26). Using data from the Dr Woosley, Gough and Prataomo created a visualisation that teaches the public on the impact of rising temperatures on the survivability of young corals. The designers utilised raw data and research articles as tools to assist them to grasp the scientific knowledge in this semantic technique of cooperation between artists and scientists. The semantic style of cooperation enabled the artists to meet with Woolsey to develop a common syntax through which they learnt about the scientific data's source. This enabled the scientist to identify her level of expertise in the field and grounded the visualisation in that information. Negotiating the language barrier allowed the creative practitioners to have a better understanding of the data gathering and its ramifications. This conversation allowed the artists to comprehend the facts, which in turn created the production of the artwork (Gough et al., 2016, p. 26). Woolsey's data is easily shown using an interactional table in Reefs on the Edge. A Tangible User Interface controls an abstract representation of the data shown onto the tabletop (de Bérginy et al, 2014, p. 452). The scientist was asked for their opinion during the development of the visuals and interactive table, as well as the design of the physical computer control system and how it would assist the audience connect with the work (Gough et al, 2016 p. 26). This interface uses physical items that are similar to real world objects to register familiarity within the user. Tangible Bits is the term that Professor of Media Arts and Sciences at the MIT Media Laboratory Hiroshi Ishii uses to describe this notion. Tangible Bits' aim is to act as a bridge between internet and the physical world. According to Ishii, Tangible Bits have the following characteristics: interactive surfaces, coupling of bits and atoms and ambient media (Ishii, 2008, pp. xix-xx). The user interface built by Gough and Pratomo, together with the work of the other collaborators, utilised the ability of all parties involved. This partnership resulted in a unique and appealing display that enabled a non-expert audience to interact with data in a unique and new manner. The *Reefs on the Edge* installation was on display in over six locations, including two at Sydney's Macleay Museum, where it drew over 14,000 visitors. In addition, the video's underwater imagery was shown in Berlin. These exhibits drew big crowds, generating widespread interest and participation in the community.

InterANTARCTICA (de Bérigny, 2008) is another example of artwork that incorporates both TUI and climate change imagery, which was also directed by Caitilin de Bérigny who collaborated with other artists and designers. This installation is based on the involvement of the audience. Viewers may interact with tangible items to experience several future possibilities for global CO_2 emissions. The interactive elements: visuals and sound, are immediately influenced by the user's interaction with the

TUI items. As a result, viewers are immersed and experience multimodal sensations via hand motion activated sound and vision (sight, sound, and touch). As a result, the interactive environment engages a variety of senses. By submerging the individual in the artwork and relying on interaction from participants, this artwork breaks down the distance psychological climate barrier, by physically placing the participants inside the space and their actions depict the negative impacts of CO_2 emissions. This concept of individual emissions having an impact on our planet can be an idea that is taken away by the audience after they leave the artwork. This work is a *syntactic* method of working, the artists and designers used scientific data without a direct collaboration with experts, this can be an effective way of indirect collaboration as the information is readily available on the internet.

Adaptation Projects

There must be caution when creating works that follow a theme of climate change and our future. Apocalyptic scenarios are just as likely to inspire helplessness as they are to inspire action. After the initial horror of facing an apocalyptic picture of the future, we swiftly find ourselves re-adapting to what we consider normal living in the actual world of our present, where indicators of imminent disaster seldom appear. Apocalypse may easily become just another sort of entertainment, a fleeting excursion into terror and fear from which we return to our regular lives mostly unaffected. Apocalyptic imagery can strengthen the 'doom' psychological barrier, therefore artworks that explore adaptation to climate change can be effective and offer a sense of hope. Imagination combined with creativity can propose new discussions and ideas about how we will adapt to a changing planet. Jennifer Gabrys, chair of culture, media and environment, and professor Kathryn Yusoff comment:

> *Climate futures arguably require approaches that are not only characterized by calculability and risk, but also mobilize imaginative acts that open new spaces and practices for dealing with the effects of living with uncertain futures* (2011, p. 518).

Imagination can facilitate a way of thinking and dreaming the future, and this can include reimagining our homes and communities. Artists can collaborate with scientists to result in adaptation to climate change projects, which can explore elements such as housing, energy, and food post-global warming. 'Eco Art 'movement founders, Helen Mayer Harrison, and Newton Harrison's exhibition *Greenhouse Britain* (Harrison and Harrison, 2007) propose a solution to all three of these factors.

The duo believes that global climate change's potential consequences are so 'compelling... catastrophic [and] destabilizing' (Harrison and Harrison, 2007, p.3) that artists 'voice must be heard in this discussion. This installation was constructed of 5 parts, the first consists of a 13-foot-long replica of the British Isles. Rivers and coastal seas are projected onto it, rising in 2 meter increments up to 16 meters in reaction to storm surge. The ten-minute audio narration asks: "How would one retreat with comparable grace?" in response to the fact that the waves will rise smoothly. It suggests that climate change is not good or bad news, but that it could be adapted to and learn lessons from. The second part *On the Upward Movement of People*, envisions a 9,000-person settlement surrounded by ecosystemically altered land that absorbs the settlement's local carbon footprint. Part three is *In Defence of the city of Bristol,* a three-minute film that recommends using the Avon River and the Avon Gorge in an innovative way to defend and save Bristol. *The Lea Valley: On the Upward Movement of Planning* is the fourth part of this installation, it is (in collaboration with APG architects) takes issue with ongoing development of the Thames estuary which proposes redesigning the 1,000-square-mile Lea Valley watershed. *The Vertical Promenade* is the last part of this exhibition, originally from a collaboration with ATOPIA architects. This project is inspired by a small-town main street, where the civic, social, and economic qualities are contained. The design is a 150-story, 5,000-person, vertically-designed community based on the notion of settlement, where ecosystemic thought drives design rather than traditional development approaches.

.This project started from an invitation from artist and activist David Haley, senior researcher at Manchester Metropolitan University, to study the effects of rising sea levels in Britain and looked at the possibility of relocating communities to higher ground in a deliberate, long-term manner (Fremantle, 2018, p. 2). In this project, the seas become a key player in guiding cultural, economic, and design initiatives for alternate habitats. Harrison's maps include a worst-case scenario of fast water rise and significant population relocation, which leads to plans for high-density bio-diverse towers in the Lea River Valley. Forests would replace any vast urban expansion, serving as carbon sinks and water storage for the watershed. Proposals for living in managed retreats, from London to a Pennine village, might be considered as scenarios that unfold a series of speculative (science informed) possibilities, rather than answers to the problem of climate change. These kinds of initiatives raise concerns about how communities, economics, and politics may change or be recast in these circumstances. Climate change is psychologically distant to us and, art, as environmentalist Bill McKibben has argued, aids us in registering events and situations that would otherwise be too large and cumbersome to grasp (McKibben, 2005). Art provides us with mental pictures that enable us to act (McKibben, 2005). This project provides us with visual imagery of a world that we cannot currently see and shows us what is possible. While this collaboration between the artists, scientists and architects can be described as a *semantic* boundary crossover, this project can also be referred to as a *pragmatic* approach. According to Carlile, pragmatically transforming knowledge *'refers to a process of altering current knowledge creating new knowledge, and validating it within each function and collectively across functions*' (Carlile, 2002, p. 445). Collaborations between the imagination and creativity of the Harrison's and the scientific experts resulted in the previously mentioned art works. By using the scientific data of proposed sea level rises and carbon sink statistics, the artists worked together with architects to create a hypothesised structure that a community can live in and survive climate change. Global warming is not envisioned as something that could teach us a tragic lesson in an artistic environment. Global warming is inside our cultural practices and everyday lives, rather than distanced as a global force of change. In this light, climate change is something to which we all participate, and it is engrained in our everyday lives (Yusoff and Gabrys, 2011, p. 523). This vision of climate change on a more local scale secures its place in the sphere of personal and societal action. *Greenhouse Britain* removes the psychological barrier of doom as it offers a proposition of a society that adapts to climate change, it also can dissect the distance barrier: adaptation is conveyed in a local environment, and it can include the individual viewing the work. The barrier of identity could also be broken down but that depends if the viewer has biased assimilation, where their cultural identity can take precedence over the facts. Per Espen Stoknes suggests that in order to gain strength against *the 5 D's* (psychological barriers of climate change), we must

> *Abandon linear antagonism, us versus them. Instead, let's move more with the flow of the human psyche. People have to want to live in a climate-friendly society because they see it as better, not because they get scared or instructed into it.*
>
> (Stokes, 2015, p. 84).

The notion of hypothesising how future communities can look like has been a theme of artworks since the 'Eco Movement 'in the late 1960s. These artworks can portray idealistic, utopian villages. Patricia Johanson, initially a minimalist painter, became interested in living material while creating geometric gardens. Her drawing *Living Apartment Houses* (Johanson, 1969) consists of huge urban buildings that are shown as undulating terraces clothed in green structures that integrate nicely with their forest-dwelling environment, rather than as skyscrapers isolated from nature. Johanson recognised the ecological advantages of green roofs, which create microenvironments for vegetation, birds, and other wildlife, as well as minimise floods via rainwater absorption, long before they were ever discussed in North America. Green roofs are being praised for their energy-saving capabilities, particularly their insulating value and capacity to mitigate the urban heat island effect, thanks to growing worries about global warming. As artist and author Caffyn Kelley observes, Johanson seeks to 'shift viewers' attention from the created object to the world unfolding inside and around it' (Kelley, 2006, p.71) Johanson's art expresses the aspiration for a better world—a more compassionate, habitable, and beautiful world—by visualising the powerful feelings so frequently absent from the environmental conversation. Johanson's illustrations hint to a kind of environmental politics that aims not just to postpone the day of reckoning, but also to anticipate the potential of human communities crafting a brighter future for themselves and other planet dwellers.

Her *Living Apartment Houses* drawing visualises what could be in a future where we cooperate with our planet and all organisms that live here, to some people it could be a better alternative to current circumstances and even start conversations on *what* a better society could look like. Rather than concentrating just on quantitative issues like improving energy efficiency and lowering carbon emissions (all of which are important), environmental reform can also provide a broader prospect of qualitative improvement in human existence. Instead of relying exclusively on the dread of the impending apocalypse for emotional appeal, it should also imagine a future where beauty is more closely related to everyday life, where humans are able to build stronger ties with each other and along with the natural environment that nourishes them. By combining creativity with imagination, artists can envisage a healthier and preferable way of life, thus coinciding with Per Espen Stoknes advice that to break down psychological barriers the public need to *want* a different, climate-friendly world.

While artistic, adaptive propositions can envision utopian, ecological societies, some artworks focus on creating self-sufficient mobile constructions. Artist Mary Mattingly has several projects which have focal points of architecture that is sustainable, and that are adaptable to our changing climate. After discovering that in New York it is illegal to cultivate vegetables for free community use on public land, she immediately thought of NYC's open waterbodies as a way of bringing fresh vegetables to more locations throughout the five boroughs, since using land was not an option. From this thinking came *Swale* (Mattingly, 2016) a floating public ecosystem garden, built upon a reclaimed barge. The garden measured 130-by-40 feet and it was the result of the idea to grow an edible plant forest on the ocean to get over the regulations and allow people to get food for free. Describing the project as *'a tool to advocate for policy change'* (Mattingly, 2016) the main objective of *Swale* is not only about creating an independent zone on the sea; it is also about foreshadowing what can happen with fresh food and public area on the land.

Mattingly had previously constructed a number of aquatic self-sustaining habitats like *Wetland* (Mattingly, 2014) and *Waterpod* (Mattingly, 2009). Another adaptive project of Mattingly is the *Flock House Project* (Mattingly, 2012), which was comprised of three self-contained ecosystems and movable, sculptural public environments, and was displayed in different urban areas. Discussing the instabilities of the environment, politics and economics within cities, Mattingly suggests this project is *'a bridge across socio-political boundaries of perimeter, property and policy'* (Mattingly, 2012, p. 5). These self-sufficient structures are conceptualised as liveable in the sea, sky and on land, well suited to conditions changing due to climate change. The apartments were made using reused materials and were tested by temporary tenants and produced utilising open-source blueprints, they pushed for more people to use natural systems like rainwater collecting, urban agriculture, and solar energy (Mattingly, 2012, pp. 16-17). This project's techniques of construction and installation were developed in partnership with Appropedia.org, a group of people devoted to the use of acceptable technology (Mattingly, 2012, p. 5). The *Flock House Project* questions *'what if mobile, self-sufficient living units were the building blocks of future cities? What if boundaries were permeable?'* (Mattingly, 2012, p. 5) and this design highlights that this is a future possibility as a way of surviving on a planet with raised sea levels.

While this project amplifies communal connection, adaptability, educational wonder, and creative inquiry through planned activities and programmes, these sculptures could be perceived as an off-putting and context lacking version of futuristic living. Examining the *Flock House Project*, Gabrys and Yusoff introduce Peder Anker, a historian of science and design and his opinion on autonomous architecture. Anker suggested that since the 1960s, a variety of 'ecological architecture' initiatives has put up solutions for sustainable housing that are based on dubious parallels to fully independent or spaceship technology and these ideas hinder our capacity to assess how life is becoming increasingly integrated in terms of cultural and political issues (Anker, 2005, cited in Gabrys and Yusoff, 2011, p. 522). Gabrys and Yusoff then explain that contemporary artists including Mary Mattingly took inspiration from these projects to create adaptation to climate change artworks and propose that there is a concern with the politics of habitable and liveable prospects. (Gabrys and Yusoff, 2011, pp. 523-524). The *Flock House* does highlight possible technologies that cope with the scarcity of resources and infrastructure failure however: Gabrys and Yusoff explain that *'these technologies are packaged in a self-contained mobile architecture that lacks context'* and these methods are better fulfilled via more in-depth contacts with the political and social ties that enable survival while being ethical (Gabrys and Yusoff, 2011, p.523-524). Climate change will affect all humankind differently, and adaptation projects should be localised to a specific area so that the design is relevant to that place, and the people that inhabit it. Relating back to Per Espen Stoknes 'suggestions to break down 'the five D's', we can look at the self-sufficient, individual units such as the *Flock House* as a depiction of the future that is bleak and unappealing. A sense of community can be a major element of humankind's existence: a government survey in 2021 reported that 65% of the public felt that they 'very strongly 'or 'fairly strongly 'belong to their immediate neighbourhood (Department for Digital, Media, Culture & Sport, 2021). This continues an increasing trend in the share of people who firmly believe they belong to their neighbourhood, rising from 58% in 2013 (Department for Digital, Media, Culture & Sport, 2021). Artistic adaptation projects need to relate their ideas to what is important to society at that given time, to be relevant and intriguing. By ignoring culture and politics, living unit proposals can be viewed as apocalyptic, they evoke fear and suggest that surviving rising sea levels will include members of society stranded floating on individual barges in open areas of water stripped of community relationships and wellbeing, strengthening the 'doom' psychological barrier that blocks climate message. Discussing climate change storytelling, Stoknes tells us that *'Only through new, attractive stories that we want to identify with will we start to reconsider the scientific facts*' (Stoknes, 2015, p. 149). He encourages us to steer clear from apocalyptic portrayals and include green growth, happiness and the good life, stewardship and ethics, rewilding, and ecological restoration (Stoknes, 2015, p. 149). Although catastrophic imagery of climate change can catch the public's attention, it does not captivate individual engagement with climate change and could possibly activate barriers. Social scientist Irene Lorenzoni who specialises in climate change engagement, Doctor of Philosophy Sophie Day, and Professor of Psychology Lorraine Whitmarsh suggest that denial is expressed by public when they think about climate change (Lorenzoni et al. 2007, p. 453). If an adaptation project is localised to a group of individuals, then it can promote a more personal story telling of climate change. Global warming can appear more relevant to those individuals, breaking the distance and denial psychological barrier. Positive adaptation projects can offer a sense of hope and even excitement about the future, these projects can be a symbol of light during dark times. The Futerra Sustainability Communications agency states that

> *At almost every turning point in human history, when things have looked the bleakest, extraordinary people have seen a different way forward. Compelling visions of 'better 'have inspired us to overcome massive odds before.*
> (Futerra Sustainability Communications, 2010, p. 10).

By providing visual, positive imagery we can encourage the public that climate change may be an opportunity to change our world for the better and inspire us to take action to help fuel that change. Even though climate change is such a broad and possibly overwhelming topic for some, visualising optimistic futures can aid the phenomenon called the 'availability heuristic 'which was introduced by behavioural scientists Amos Tversky and Daniel Kahneman. The availability heuristic suggests that people rely on examples of an event that can be envisioned or remembered, when determining the possibility or frequency of an occurrence (Tversky and Kahneman, 1973, p. 231). This explains that the more perceivable imagery of climate-friendly futures the public view, the higher chance they will believe that it is possible to live in a world that takes care of its planet and in turn, takes care of its inhabitants. Following this, psychological climate barriers can be broken down as 'distance' and 'doom' are counteracted with personal, positive envisions. However, the availability heuristic can impact negatively as the more apocalyptic imagery people observe the more likely are they to believe that climate change will result in the collapse of humankind. Such a belief may strengthen the 'doom' barrier resulting in people wishing to avoid the topic of climate change. News reports continuously broadcast current impacts of global warming such as natural disasters, during 2021 in America alone there were 18 weather/climate disasters that cost over 1 billion dollars each which is an increase from an average of 6.3 climate disasters during the 2010s (NCEI, 2021). With increasing numbers of floods, hurricanes, forest fires comes more news coverage. Therefore, there is a need for alternative, positive scenarios to encourage individual thinking that global warming is not an apocalyptic reality but an opportunity to change ways of society for the better, for humankind and the planet.

Conclusion

This book has analysed the relationship between society and science in the concept of climate change and clarified that there is a gap in communication: a result of the public not understanding science, scepticism, or biased assimilation. To bridge this gap between climate change knowledge and society, we can use art and science collaborations to educate about global warming in an accessible (non-expert user visualisation) and interactive (tangible user interface) manner, which can help break down the psychological barriers we face when discussing climate change. These projects can immerse an individual into an experience that can register both modes of thinking: cognitive and emotional, aiding environmentally friendly behaviours. By assessing several case studies, this research identified boundary objects that occur when artists and scientists collaborate on the topic of climate change, these boundary objects can be categorised as syntactic, semantic, and pragmatic. The pragmatic version of a boundary object is most useful for engaging the public with climate knowledge as these artworks can offer new information by combining statistics with imagination to propose adaptive scenarios that are not offered from science alone. Adaptation projects must be appealing to break down psychological barriers, they can do this by including elements of society that matter such as well-being, community, and a sense of belonging. Projects that envision future adaptation to climate change as self-sustaining individual living units lack these important elements and these projects can appear apocalyptic and off-putting and could therefore strengthen the 'doom' psychological barrier. A positive adaptation to climate change installation that included an interactive mode could be an effective way to encourage the public to think about our changing planet without frightening them. There would be great use to have more social science methodology investigate the impact that climate art has on individuals referring to if and how their behaviours change. We can continue to learn how effective art and science collaborations are for communicating climate change issues, and using art as a tool we can break down psychological barriers. Art does not only visualise scientific data, but it can also register emotions and provide us with inspiration, it captures our imaginations and envisions a better world:

> *Art, it is said, is not a mirror, but a hammer: it does not reflect, it shapes.*
>
> (Trotsky, 1924, p. 120)

Eilidh Guthrie

References

Buckland, D., 2012. 'Climate is culture.' *Nature Clim Change* 2, pp. 137–140
[online] Available at: http://geodesy.unr.edu/hanspeterplag/library/documents/201203_Buckland_Nature_climate_change.pdf [Accessed 10 October 2021].

Bullot, N. J., 2014. *The Functions of Environmental Art*. Leonardo [online] Available at: https://research-management.mq.edu.au/ws/portalfiles/portal/62296445/Publisher+version+%28open+access%29.pdf [Accessed 7 January 2022].

Carbon Brief., 2021. *Analysis: UK is now halfway to meeting its 'net-zero emissions' target - Carbon Brief*. [online] Available at: https://www.carbonbrief.org/analysis-uk-is-now-halfway-to-meeting-its-net-zero-emissions-target [Accessed 15 November 2021].

Carlile, P., 2002. 'A Pragmatic View of Knowledge and Boundaries: Boundary Objects in New Product Development.' *Organization Science*, 13(4), pp.442-455.

Corner, A., Whitmarsh, L. and Xenias, D., 2012. 'Uncertainty, scepticism and attitudes towards climate change: biased assimilation and attitude polarisation', *Climatic change*, 114(3), pp. 463–478.

Cross, N. (2006) *Designerly Ways of Knowing*. 1. Aufl. London: Springer Verlag London Limited. pp. 221–227.

de Bérigny, C., 2008. *interANTARCTICA*. [Installation].
de Bérigny, C., 2011. *Reefs on the Edge*. [Installation].
de Bérigny, C., Gough, P., Faleh, M., & Woolsey, E., 2014. Tangible User Interface Design for Climate Change Education in Interactive Installation Art. *Leonardo*, *47*(5), pp. 451–457.
Department for Business, Energy and Industrial Strategy., 2019. *Public attitudes to science*. [online] Available at: https://assets.publishing.service.gov.uk/government/uploads/system/uploads/attachment_data/file/905466/public-attitudes-to-science-2019.pdf [Accessed 15 November 2021]
Department for Digital, Culture, Media & Sport., 2021. *Official Statistics Neighbourhood and Community - Community Life Survey 2020/21*. Available at: https://www.gov.uk/government/statistics/community-life-survey-202021-neighbourhood-and-community/neighbourhood-and-community-community-life-survey-202021 [Accessed 15 November 2021].
Dickson, D., 2005. 'The case for a 'deficit model' of science communication.' [online] Available at: https://www.scidev.net/global/editorials/the-case-for-a-deficit-model-of-science-communic/ [Accessed 15 August 2021].
Epstein, S., 1994. 'Integration of the Cognitive and psychodynamic unconscious.' *American Psychologist,* 49(8), pp.706-724.

Fremantle, C., 2018. *Greenhouse Britain: losing ground, gaining wisdom (2006-09): case study.* [online] Available at: https://rgu-repository.worktribe.com/output/249255/greenhouse-britain-losing-ground-gaining-wisdom-2 [Accessed 15 October 2021].

Futerra Sustainability Communications., 2018. *Sizzle - The New Climate Message.* [ebook] Available at: https://www.wearefuterra.com/wp-content/uploads/2018/03/Sellthesizzle.pdf [Accessed 10 December 2021].

Goreau, T.J.F. and Hayes, R.L, 2021. *Global warming triggers coral reef bleaching tipping point.* Ambio's 50th Anniversary Collection. *Ambio,* 50(6), pp. 1137-1140.

Gough, P., Wall, C.B., and Bednarz, T., 2014. 'Affective and effective visualisation: communicating science to non-expert users.' *Pacific Visualisation Symposium (Pacific Vis.)* pp. 335-339.

Gough, P., Dunn, K., and de Bérigny, C., 2016. 'Climate Change Education through Art and Science Collaborations.' *IGI Global.*

Harrison, H. and Harrison, N., 2007. *Greenhouse Britain.* [Installation].

Harrison, N., and Harrison H., 2007. Greenhouse Britain: Losing Ground, Gaining Wisdom, Proposal Pamphlet.

Ishii, H., 2008. 'Tangible bits: beyond pixels.' *Proceedings of the 2nd international conference on tangible and embedded interaction.*

Johanson, P., 1969. *Living Apartment Houses.* [pencil and coloured pencil on paper].

Kelley, C., 2006. Art and Survival: Patricia Johanson's Environmental Projects. *Gulf Islands Institute.*

Leiserowitz, A., 2006. 'Climate Change Risk Perception and Policy Preferences: The Role of Affect, Imagery, and Values'. *Climatic Change,* 77(1), pp. 45–72.

Levin, H., 1965. Semantics of Culture. *Daedalus.* 94(1), [online] Available at: http://www.jstor.org/stable/20026892 [Accessed 13 January 2021].

Liberman, N. and Trope, Y. (2008) 'The Psychology of Transcending the Here and Now', *Science (American Association for the Advancement of Science)*, 322(5905), pp. 1201–1205. Available at: https://www.ncbi.nlm.nih.gov/pmc/articles/PMC2643344/ [Accessed 13 September 2021].

Lord, C. G., Ross, L., & Lepper, M. R., 1979. 'Biased assimilation and attitude polarization: The effects of prior theories on subsequently considered evidence.' *Journal of Personality and Social Psychology*, p. 2099.

Lorenzoni, I., Nicholson-Cole, S. A., & Whitmarsh, L., 2007. 'Barriers perceived to engaging with climate change among the UK public and their policy implications.' 17(3), *Global Environmental Change.* pp. 445-459.

Mattingly, M., 2009. *Waterpod.* [Sculpture].

Mattingly, M., 2012. *Flock House Project.* [Sculpture].

Mattingly, M., 2012. *Flock House.* [ebook] Available at: https://marymattingly.com/pdfs/FHBookTest2.pdf [Accessed 5 November 2021]

Mattingly, M., 2014. *WetLand*. [Sculpture].
Mattingly, M., 2016. *Mary Mattingly - Swale*. [online] Marymattingly.com. Available at: https://marymattingly.com/html/MATTINGLYSwale.html [Accessed 5 November 2021].
Mattingly, M., 2016. *Swale*. [Public Artwork: Floating Food Forest].
McKibben, B., 2005. 'What the Warming World Needs Now is Art, Sweet Art' [online] Available at: https://grist.org/article/mckibben-imagine/ [Accessed 11 December 2021]
Milfont, T.L., 2010. 'Global warming, climate change and human psychology.' In V. Corral Verdugo, C.H. García-Cadena, and M. Frías-Arment. *Psychological approaches to sustainability: Current trends in theory, research and practice.* New York. Nova Science Publishers.
Pinsky, M., 2017. *Pollution Pods*. [Installation].
Pinsky, M. 2017. Pollution Pods. Retrieved from https://www.climart.info/pollutionpods [Accessed 10 October 2021].
Pinsky, M., and Sommer, L., 2020. 'Pollution Pods: can art change people's perception of climate change and air pollution?' [online] pp. 90-95. Available at: https://journals.openedition.org/factsreports/6161[Accessed 12 October 2021].

Pouliot, C. and Godbout, J. (2014) 'Thinking outside the "knowledge deficit" box: Scientists could achieve more fulfilled professional lives by embracing the skills needed for effective interaction with the public', *EMBO reports*, 15(8), pp. 833–835.
Available at:
https://www.ncbi.nlm.nih.gov/pmc/articles/PMC4197039/pdf/embr0015-0833.pdf pp. 833-835. [Accessed 24 October 2021]

Spence, A., Poortinga, W. and Pidgeon, N. (2012) 'The Psychological Distance of Climate Change', *Risk analysis*, 32(6), pp. 957–972.

Snow, C. P. (Charles P)., 1959. 'The Two Cultures.' Cambridge: *Cambridge University Press*, pp. 4-9.

Star, S. and Griesemer, J., 1989. Institutional Ecology, `Translations' and Boundary Objects: Amateurs and Professionals in Berkeley's Museum of Vertebrate Zoology', *Social Studies of Science*, [online] 19(3), pp.387-420. Available at:
http://www.lchc.ucsd.edu/MCA/Mail/xmcamail.2012_08.dir/pdfMrgHgzULhA.pdf [Accessed 2 September 2021]

Stoknes, Per., 2015. *What We Think About When We Try Not To Think About Global Warming*. Hartford: Chelsea Green Publishing. pp. 81-84.

Trotsky, L., 1924. Literature and Revolution. New York: *Pathfinder Press,* p 120.

Tversky, A., and Kahneman, D., 1973. 'Availability: A Heuristic for Judging Frequency and Probability', *Cognitive Psychology*, 5, pp. 207-232.

Woolsey, E., 2012. Self-fertilization suppresses thermal tolerance in embryos of reef-building coral. *Proceedings of the 12th International Coral Reef Symposium*, Cairns, Australia. [online] Available at: https://www.icrs2012.com/proceedings/manuscripts/ICRS2012_12A_5.pdf [Accessed 13 September 2021].

Yusoff, K. and Gabrys, J., 2011. 'Climate change and the imagination', *Wiley interdisciplinary reviews. Climate change,* 2(4), [online] pp. 516-530. Available at: https://wires.onlinelibrary.wiley.com/doi/epdf/10.1002/wcc.117?saml_referrer [Accessed 27 September 2021].

Eilidh Guthrie

Artist's images

The following images are work displayed by Eilidh Guthrie for her degree show at the Duncan of Jordanstone College of Art and Design, Scotland, 2022.

This multimedia installation explores Eilidh's journey of mortality salience and her solace in finding a parallel between port-mortem bodies and trees.

Through clay, bronze and wood, she explored the taboo topic of death.

Finding solace in knowing that her energy and all living organisms of the forest will return to the earth one day, our limbs, tree limbs, all returning after life -their decomposition becoming nutritional distribution. The "Forest Breathing", perpetually maintains the conditions required for all life. Where tree burrs become the bloated hybrid bodies, the sculpture studio becomes the post-mortem examination, the kiln, a resurrection through fire and earth.

Eilidh Guthrie

Art & Science Collaborations

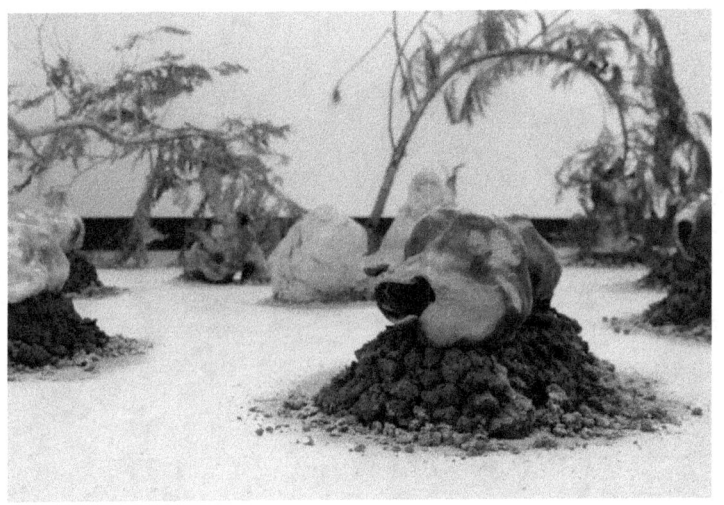

Eilidh Guthrie

Art & Science Collaborations

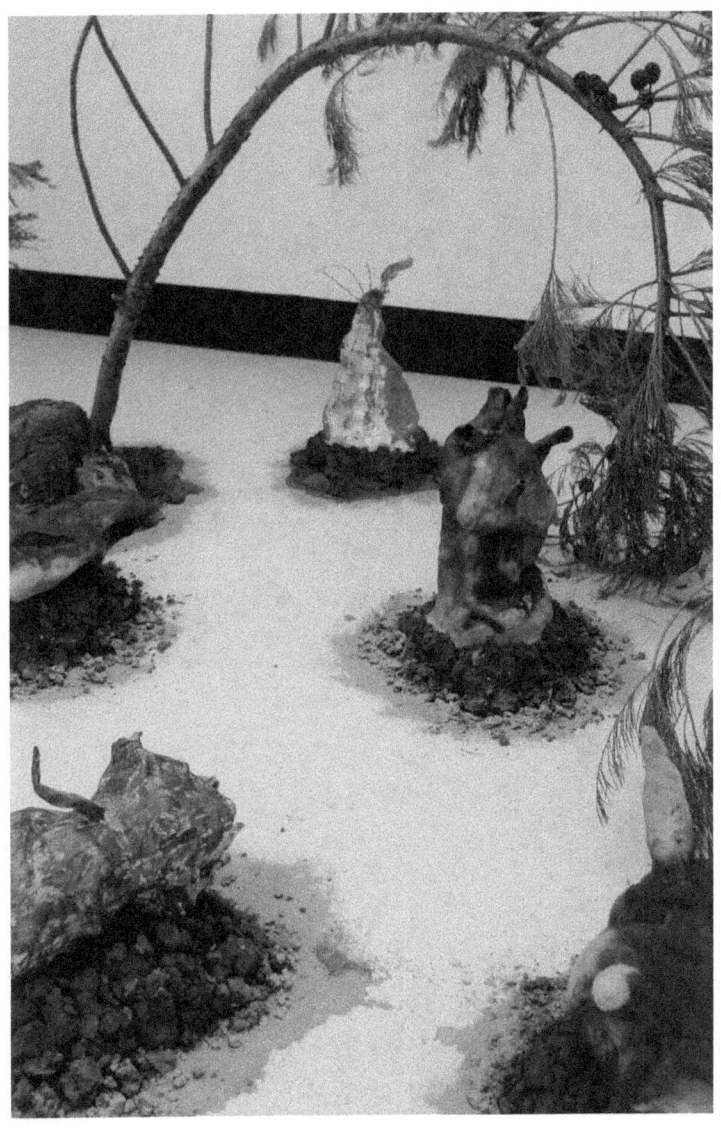

Eilidh Guthrie

Art & Science Collaborations

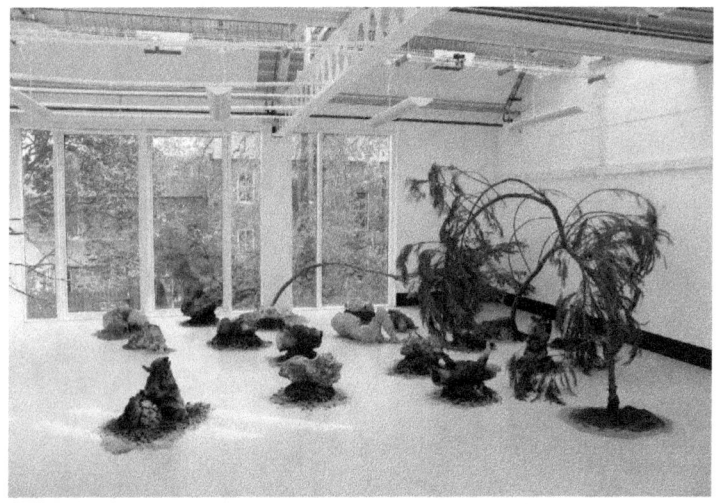

Eilidh Guthrie

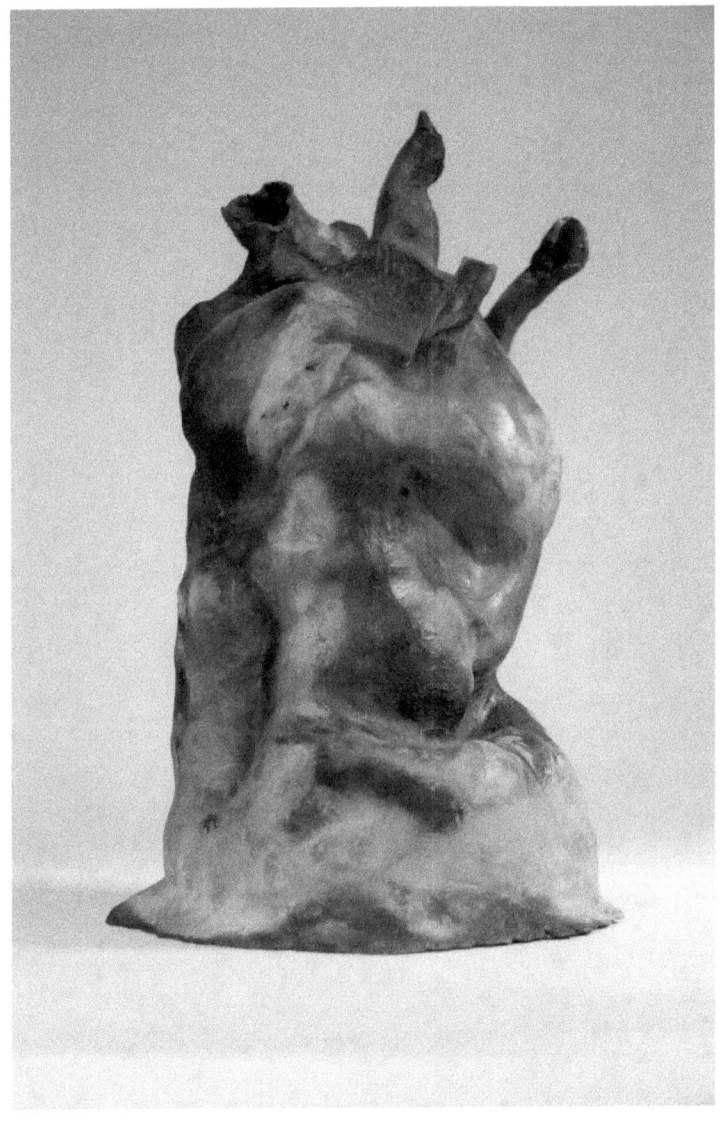

Eilidh Guthrie

Art & Science Collaborations

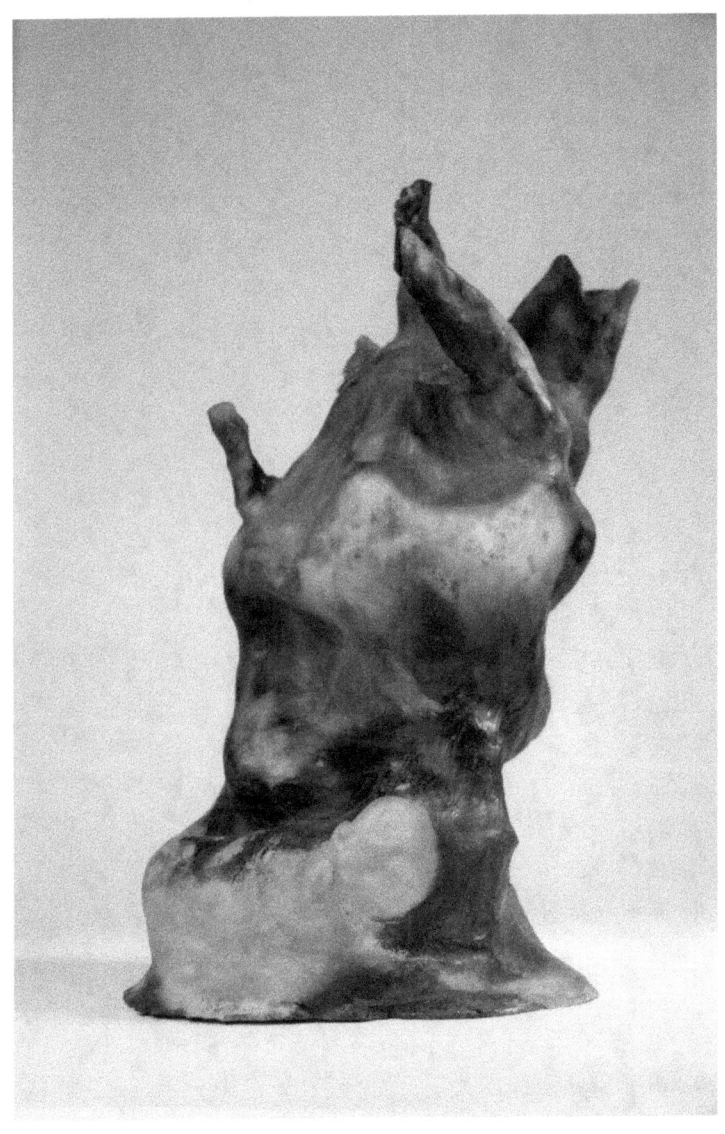

Eilidh Guthrie

Art & Science Collaborations

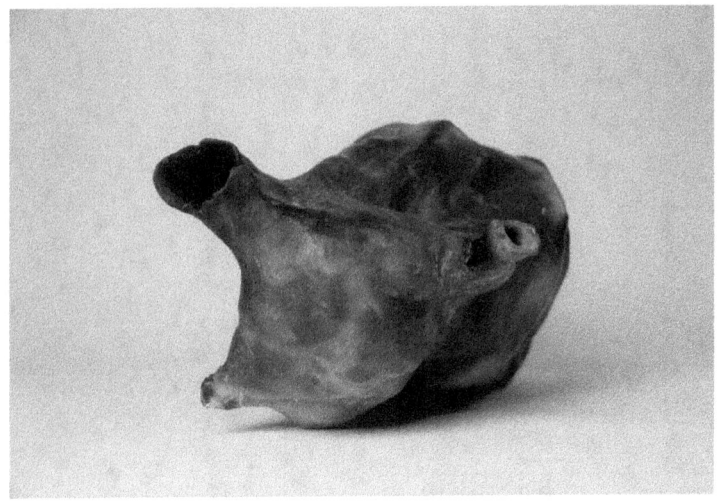

Eilidh Guthrie

Art & Science Collaborations

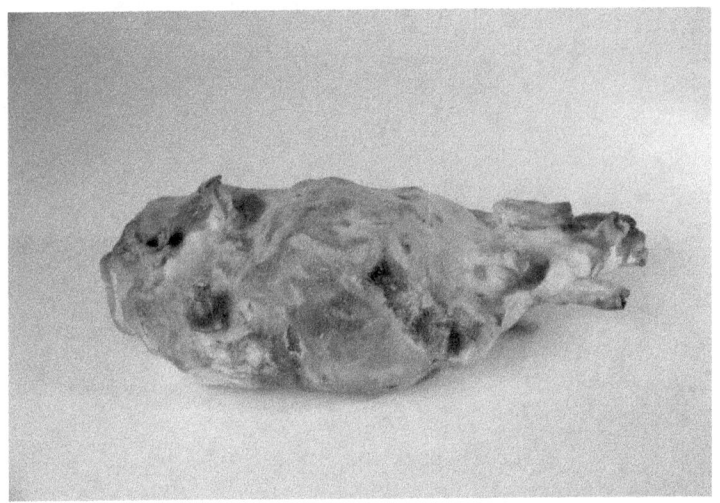

Eilidh Guthrie

Art & Science Collaborations

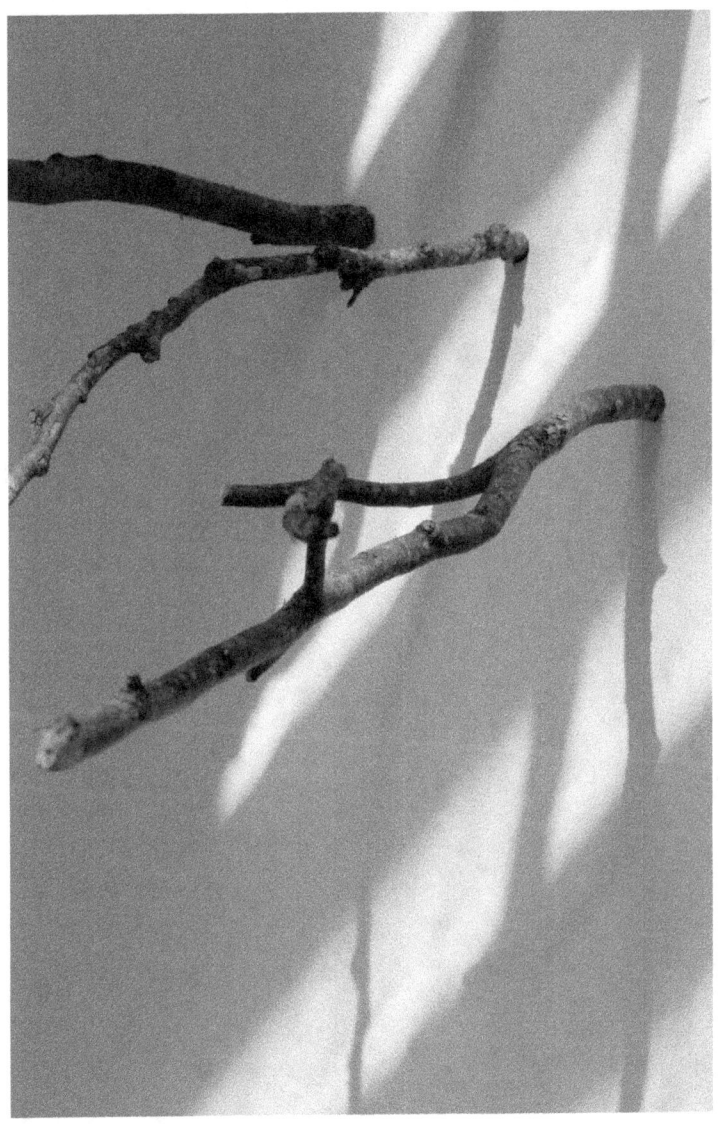

Eilidh Guthrie

Art & Science Collaborations

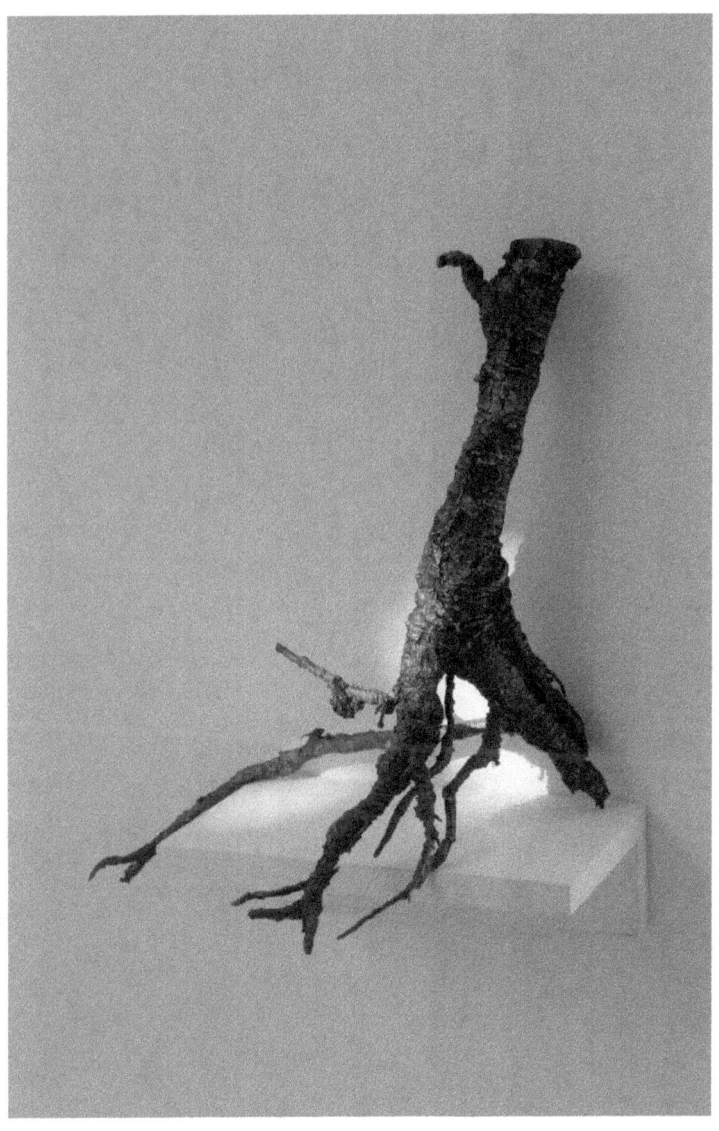

Eilidh Guthrie

Acknowledgements

I'm extremely grateful to my dissertation supervisor, Gair Dunlop, whose support and knowledge guided me from start to finish in writing this book. I would like to extend my sincere thanks to Helen Gorrill, for her motivation, patience and expertise in writing and publishing and to BOOM Graduates for this amazing opportunity.

Words cannot express my gratitude to my partner Ali, who has encouraged me to finish this degree through the thousands of complete meltdowns. Thank you for assisting me in whatever way you could, from allowing me to cover you in found fishing gear in the bath or driving me back and forth to Invergowrie to dig clay at the beach (don't worry, I'll get you a pair of wellies and a spade for next time).

Lastly, I could not have undertaken this journey without my phenomenal parents. From building me a summerhouse in the garden so I could continue to practice art for my

degree during the pandemic, allowing me to dry my questionable clay baby heads dry around the fire and to allow me to pursue whatever mad dream pops into my head
 - I love you both so much.

Art & Science Collaborations

BOOM!

This book was originally submitted s a dissertation in partial fulfilment of the requirements of a Bachelor of Arts (Hons) degree in Fine Art at the Duncan of Jordanstone College of Art and Design, the University of Dundee, in 2022.

Eilidh Guthrie

A note about Boom Graduates

We propel graduates forward so they can make their mark on the world - we push the boundaries, share brilliant ideas and inspire possibility. We publish dissertations as books, presented gift-boxed at graduation ceremonies, delivering brand-new research to the world quicker than anyone else. We plant trees for every commissioned book sold, and give our Boom graduates the chance to profit-share from their brilliant ideas. Furthermore we donate the majority of our profits to funding research and scholarship for disadvantaged students who wouldn't normally be able to attend university. Through academic excellence and environmental sustainability, *Boom Graduates* are changing the world.

We are Boom Graduates - an imprint of Boom Publications Ltd. We are a more-than-profit company, dedicating over half our profits to providing university scholarships for underprivileged students across the world. We aim to become the globe's biggest provider of such scholarships – and if like Eilidh, the author of this book, you'd also like to contribute to making the world a better place, please contact us: we publish monographs, edited books, and moreover our graduate series – Boom Graduates – are presented at graduation days across the world in archival, lined museum-quality presentation cases, engraved with the graduate's name and award.

Boom Publications are based at the Duncan of Jordanstone College of Art and Design, at the University of Dundee in Scotland. We were one of the winners of the 2022 Venture awards hosted by the Centre for Entrepreneurship, and have since been shortlisted for the Converge Challenge, a national award that brings together ambitious and creative thinkers with innovative ideas to work with Industry experts to transform their ideas into sustainable companies operating in the commercial world. We are also climate conscious and work with agencies to plant a tree for each and every book commissioned, offsetting thousands of tonnes of carbon each year. Follow us on social media to watch our forest grow @boomgraduates.

Thank you for contributing by purchasing this book. Please visit our catalogues on www.boompublications.com.

Eilidh Guthrie

Notes

Eilidh Guthrie

Art & Science Collaborations

Eilidh Guthrie

Art & Science Collaborations

Eilidh Guthrie

Art & Science Collaborations

Eilidh Guthrie

www.ingramcontent.com/pod-product-compliance
Lightning Source LLC
Chambersburg PA
CBHW071423210526
45465CB00001B/502